The Third Temple and the Final Harvest

A prophetic look at what's just around the corner!

Malachi 3 and 4 will be re-fulfilled — during the coming final outpouring, on the day that God acts.

Learn how to be part of the coming final awakening.

Charles Pretlow

The Third Temple and the Final Harvest
A prophetic look at what's just around the corner!
January 2019

ISBN 978-1-943412-10-5

Published by
Wilderness Voice Publishing
PO Box 857
Canon City, CO 81215

"A voice crying in the wilderness –
proclaiming the good news of the coming Kingdom!"

Contents

Introduction

There are many interpretations concerning end-of-this-age events. However, there is only one that is correct. This short commentary describes the true scenario of Christ's second coming.

Importantly, this commentary introduces the basic Biblical principles that you need to understand and embrace in order to start your journey with Christ, if you haven't already. A journey that will lead you to assurance that you are not deceived, are truly saved, and how to victoriously endure to the end of the coming troubles.

Christ warned of this time that is now coming upon us, to watch and not be weighed down and be asleep to the coming worldwide deception.

Satan, through his antichrist, will succeed in deceiving the whole world and, if possible, God's true servants.

Great trouble is about to befall America and the world. The question we all must ask ourselves and confer with the Lord about is, "Will I be able to endure to the end and escape the coming trouble before Christ's appearance?"

Jesus was clear about the difficulties of the hour that is now coming upon us. For "the unprepared" the impending deception and trouble will come like a trap:

"But watch yourselves lest your hearts be weighed down with dissipation and drunkenness and cares of this life, and that day come upon you suddenly like a trap. For it will come upon all who dwell on the face of the whole earth. But stay awake at all times, praying that you may have strength to escape all these

things that are going to take place, and to stand before the Son of Man" (Luke 21:34-36).

Also, to encourage us through this coming dark hour, Christ said, *"Now when these things begin to take place, straighten up and raise your heads, because your redemption is drawing near... So also, when you see these things taking place, you know that the kingdom of God is near"* (Luke 21:28-31).

God's end-of-this-age events that Jesus spoke of are accelerating with extreme intensity and frequency. The Holy Spirit is using this message and other messengers to awaken God's people to become ready.

"Stay dressed for action and keep your lamps burning, and be like men who are waiting for their master to come home from the wedding feast, so that they may open the door to him at once when he comes and knocks. Blessed are those servants whom the master finds awake when he comes" (Luke 12:35-37).

Dedication of Third Temple Altar

On Monday, December 10th, 2018 —the last day of Hanukkah, the Sanhedrin called out to 70 nations to join in the consecration of the altar for the Third Temple. A full-dress reenactment of the daily sacrifice was held, to include a sacrificed sheep.

This reenactment is the first daily sacrifice in almost 2,000 years, held at the wailing wall at the temple mount. All the ancient instruments and pieces used in the traditional daily sacrifice have been made and are ready to install, once the Third Temple is constructed.

This is a very significant event in these last days and the fulfillment of prophesy, pointing to the fulfilment of more end-of-the-age prophesies that are *just around the corner*.

The Third Temple will soon be built upon the temple mount next to the dome of the rock.

Few Christians heard of this enactment of the daily sacrifice on December 10th, 2018 let alone grasp the significance.

The Antichrist's Temple Is Ready to Be Constructed

The soon to be revealed antichrist, disguised as Israel's long-time-in-coming messiah, will make his global debut. This savior of Israel will be the man of lawlessness, who will become Satan's puppet to rule the world. Through the antichrist rule, Satan will succeed in deceiving the whole world and bring temporary false peace to Israel and the world.

Most Christians believe they will not live to see the antichrist, or they will be raptured to safety by the Lord before his grand entrance on the world stage.

However, the coming of the Lord will occur after the antichrist is revealed and begins his rule, just as the Apostle Paul described, *"Let no one deceive you in any way. For that day [Christ's appearance] will not come, unless the rebellion comes first, and the man of lawlessness is revealed, the son of destruction, who opposes and exalts himself against every so-called god or object of worship, so that he takes his seat in the temple of God, proclaiming himself to be God"* (2 Thessalonians 2:3-4).

Of course, Jesus describes this coming event as the antichrist, who is the *abomination of desolation*, standing in the Holy Place. Jesus goes on in Matthew 24 explaining that this future event that is to take place in Israel's Temple will ignite the beginning of the end and the start of the Great Tribulation. *"For then there will be great tribulation, such as has not been from the beginning of the world until now, no, and never will be. And if those days had not been cut short, no human being would be saved. But for the sake of the elect those days will be cut short"* (Matthew 24:21-22).

Israel will not be converted to the true Christ through the efforts of Christianity. Every sincere Christian must accept this truth now, because the time we have remaining to prepare is running short. To repeat, the Apostle Paul warns about the second coming of Christ saying, *let no one deceive you in any way.*

Unfortunately, most believers are grossly deceived!

Israel Is Still On-The-Outs with the Lord

Israel fell away from God's protection when they rejected Christ as their Messiah. For this, Jerusalem and the Second Temple were destroyed and Israel, as a people, became scattered and taken into captivity.

By rejecting Christ as their Savior, the Jewish people fell out of God's favor and were disbursed throughout the world as a people without a nation. However, as prophesied in Scripture, Israel was born anew and became a nation once again in 1948.

Since then Jews throughout the world have been drawn back to the land of Palestine, to live together as a people—to once again be recognized by the world as the nation of Israel. Since then Israel, as a new nation, has been constantly attacked and harassed—and looking for a savior, as promised in Scripture. When Christ is revealed, the whole world will witness his coming with the clouds. That is when Israel will cry out to Christ as a people. They will then, and only then, realize that Christ is their true Messiah—the Son of God who they rejected and pierced.

Behold, he is coming with the clouds, and every eye will see him, even those who pierced him, and all tribes of the earth will wail on account of him.

Revelation 1:7

Unfortunately, until Christ's appearance in the clouds, Israel will continue to reject Christ as their Savior and wholeheartedly look for another to come as their messiah. Thus, they continue to be deceived and will soon embrace the antichrist as their messiah and give him homage, allowing him to be seated in the Holy Place within the Third Temple. *These Biblical prophesies are about to be fulfilled.*

The soon to be constructed Third Temple is not God's temple but a replica of the temple in Scripture made by the Jewish leaders of Israel, who are still in rebellion against their true Messiah.

Jesus replaced the temple worship system with his sacrifice, resurrection, and his accent to the right hand of God—and by sending the Holy Spirit to abide in the hearts of all genuine believers, Jew and Gentile alike.

God's Spirit dwells in the hearts and lives of those who believe and obey Christ. True Christians are the body of Christ on earth and are the Temple of the Holy Spirit. Not the Third Temple about to be built in Jerusalem.

However, God's true temple, the Christian Church is fouled up, corrupt, impure, divided, and in bondage to the love of this world—just as Israel's Temple system at Christ's first coming.

Jesus, at his first coming went into the Second Temple and used a whip to chase out the money changers. So corrupt were the high priest and the Temple leaders, that Jesus bypassed them all and called common uneducated men to follow him and to become his disciples. A major part of Christ's work in his first coming was to shut down the Temple worship system, that had gone bad beyond reformation, and replace it.

God's True Temple Needs Purification

A similar purification is coming to God's true temple—that is the body of Christ. The soon to be bride of

Christ is about to be cleansed by Christ, just as the Apostle Paul prophesied: *"So that he might present the church to himself in splendor, without spot or wrinkle or any such thing, that she might be holy and without blemish"* (Ephesians 5:27).

The Christian Church system, like the Temple system, has also gone bad beyond reformation.

Through the years, since the beginning of this church age, Satan has tried to destroy Christ's Church. Unable to do so, the devil changed tactics and repeatedly sent in wolves to hijack and infiltrate most of Christianity. God raised up true leaders to reform and correct; unfortunately, most were defeated, and many were forced to come away from the false to start anew.

In general, the reformation continued with new denominations and movements to correct false doctrine and maintain purity in fellowship.

However, in these last moments of this age, false teachers, false doctrines, and false prophets walking in false spiritual power have almost completely suppressed the truth concerning how Christ will return.

Few Christians are instructed on how to become ready to endure the end-of-this-age turbulence. Christians are asleep at the darkest hour and are not prepared to endure to the end.

For the deceived but sincere believer, the coming troubles and persecution leading into the Great Tribulation will be used by God to wake up and cleanse the body of Christ. These troubles will be used by God to vet out the false Christian.

God is about to expose false movements, false prophets, and evil weeds that are hiding in church, ministry and family—that is, for the Christian who desires to know the truth and take heed.

A great division is coming—a separation between the false and the true believer.

It will not be a continuation of the reformation process but rather a coming out or coming away process. Masses of sincere Christians are about to be awakened, and in order to become ready they will have to come away from a very polluted religious system, a system that many call churchianity.

Most of Christianity has made a covenant with the world, in order to be accepted and live in harmony. Worldliness, carnal spiritualism, sin, and secret wickedness has taken over much of Christianity.

The coming persecution and troubles will end this sick marriage between Christians and the world.

The choice will become clear, where deceived denominations or fellowships will fall away from the truth completely but still hold control over the false and deceived Christian.

The foolish, false Christian will have their fate sealed and become locked out of the coming marriage between Christ and his bride—a purified Church!

In this vetting process, the true Christian will become strong in faith and realize the end is coming upon the world. It is these committed and purified Christians that God will use in the coming final harvest of souls during the Great Tribulation.

Review the Apostle Paul's warning: *"The coming of the lawless one is by the activity of Satan with all power and false signs and wonders, and with all wicked deception for those who are perishing, because they refused to love the* *truth and so be saved. Therefore God sends them a strong delusion, so that they may believe what is false, in order that all may be condemned who <u>did not believe the truth but had pleasure in unrighteousness</u>"* (2 Thessalonians 2:9-12).

Just as the high priest and the temple leaders rejected Christ's first coming, so too in these last days, most false leaders and corrupt church organizations will reject how Christ will come again. *However, many deceived leaders will repent, adhere to the truth, and be used of God in the coming final harvest.*

The false church leaders, like the false temple leaders, will make a deal with the coming antichrist government. The true believer will be powerless to correct the false and be forced to come away or end up falling away with the deceived leaders who will still be in control of many Christian churches, movements, and organizations.

Brace yourself for a great falling away just as Jesus explained. This will begin to happen before the antichrist is revealed.

Over the last fifty years much speculation and wrong interpretation of Scripture has lulled most Christians into a deep sleep. During the late 60s and early 70s great anticipation of Christ's coming became a wave of hope, but all that enthusiasm has waned.

Jesus warned of this in his parable of the Ten Virgins, where the maidens in wait fell asleep because the bridegroom was delayed (see Matthew 25:1-13).

In mercy and patience God desires to see all come to repentance, thus the end is coming, but not all at once. Christ explains: *"See that you are not led astray. For many will come in my name, saying, 'I am he!' and, 'The time is at hand!' Do not go after them. And when you hear of wars and tumults, do not be terrified, for these things must first take place, but the end will not be at once"* (Luke 21:8-9).

Knowing the Truth About What Is Coming Does Not Make One Pure and Ready
Malachi 3 and 4 Are Being Re-Fulfilled

For years Christ has been preparing true servants to bring forth sound doctrine on how to prepare for the coming kingdom. Now, as chaos and lawlessness increase, the only good news for the true believer will be the preaching and teaching of the coming kingdom and how to prepare to endure to the end.

The true believer must become strengthened in faith to endure victoriously the coming waves of troubles and persecution. Few are ready to endure to the end in this coming vetting process that will make Christ's church into a pure bride.

To help the true Christian become prepared, true servants will seemingly come from no-where and not be from the company of the famous.

Just as Christ called his first Apostles from the common people and not the temple priesthood. So again, Christ has already called his bondservants, not from the heralded leaders of today — but in secret, starting years ago.

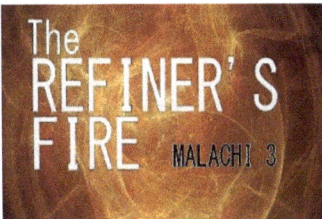

These servants are men and women of God who have spent years in the wilderness, dying to any need of reputation. These are true shepherds who know Christ and are known by him, who only serve Christ and refuse to be men pleasers.

Jesus has been refining these true servants just as it was prophesied in Malachi. This is what he did with his first Apostles and servants, and so again in these last days he has been refining and will continue to refine his true servants: *"But who can endure the day of his coming, and who can stand when he appears? For he is like a refiner's fire and like fullers' soap. He will sit as a refiner and purifier of silver, and he will purify the sons of Levi and refine them like gold and silver, and they will bring offerings in righteousness to the LORD"* (Malachi 3:2-3).

John the Baptist confirms Malachi 3, by declaring Christ's work as a purifier and refiner of his true servants: *"He will baptize you with the Holy Spirit and fire. His winnowing fork is in his hand, and he will clear his threshing floor and gather his wheat into the barn, but the chaff he will burn with unquenchable fire"* (Matthew 3:11-12).

Christ's first disciples were indeed ran-through-the-ringer. Every ounce of ill character and the love for this life was burned up within them through an unquenchable fire of trouble. The disciples despaired of life itself and were scattered, hiding from the temple leaders in fear of their own crucifixion, all while Christ suffered and was crucified.

However, Christ arose from the dead and appeared to them to their amazement. From then on, the disciples feared no man but served the risen Christ, no longer fearing death.

Even the Apostle Paul (whom Christ chose to replace Judas the betrayer) had to endure this very same grueling refiner's fire. Paul explains: *"Indeed, we felt that we had received the sentence of death. But that was to make us rely not on ourselves but on God who raises the* dead. He delivered us from such a deadly peril, and he will deliver us. On him we have set our hope that he will deliver us again" (2 Corinthians 1:9-10).

Another declaration by the Apostle Paul explains further what it means to be a true dead-to-self servant that confronts false leaders who distort the Gospel of Christ: *"As we have said before, so now I say again: If anyone is preaching to you a gospel contrary to the one you received, let him be accursed. For am I now seeking the approval of man, or of God? Or am I trying to please man? If I were still trying to please man, I would not be a servant of Christ"* (Galatians 1:9-10).

Few in leadership today allow Christ to chasten, purify, and refine their character so they can become Christlike. Most embrace a distorted Gospel and learn to take the easy way, creating an outer personality that seems Christlike.

These self-made disciples fearfully avoid entering in to a death like Christ, which allows Christlike character to take root. *"For if we have been united with him in a death like his, we shall certainly be united with him in a resurrection like his"* (Romans 6:5).

Like the Third Temple soon to be constructed, Christians are taught to build their own Christlike inner being and character, but unsuccessfully. *"Unless the LORD builds the house, those who build it labor in vain"* (Psalm 127:1).

Those who embrace the Lord's discipline, trials, and tests. Those who embrace death-to-old-self moments orchestrated by the Lord—these are the children whom God will protect and use on the day that he acts: *"They shall be mine, says the LORD of hosts, in the day when I make up my treasured possession, and I will spare them as a man spares his son who serves him. Then once more you shall see the distinction between the righteous and the wicked, between one who serves God and one who does not serve him... But for you who fear my name, the sun of righteousness shall rise with healing in its wings. You shall go out leaping like calves from the stall. And you shall tread down the wicked, for they will be ashes under the soles of your feet, on the day when I act, says the LORD of hosts"* (Malachi 3:17-18; 4:2-3).

Building Your Life on Christ's Words

How does a new Christian or longtime believer prepare for the coming end-of-this-age challenges, troubles, and turbulent times?

Bible College and special seminary courses? Study God's words over and over? Attend church regularly? Volunteer for ministry? Read books on devotion, discipleship, and on successful living for Jesus?

These activities may help in some ways, but they fall short unless they point to Christ and his discipline in everyday living—where one learns to embrace trials of faith that produce inner character transformation.

This comes only by walking out a living

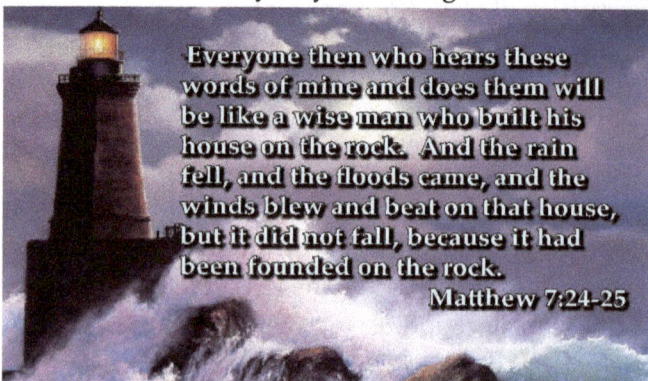

Everyone then who hears these words of mine and does them will be like a wise man who built his house on the rock. And the rain fell, and the floods came, and the winds blew and beat on that house, but it did not fall, because it had been founded on the rock.

Matthew 7:24-25

relationship with Christ, where ALL of Christ's words are understood and embraced. It is Christ who perfects our transformation—not by us doing for him but by our working with him and by Christ working in us and through us.

Simply put, Christ explains: *"Why do you call me 'Lord, Lord,' and not do what I tell you? Everyone who comes to me and hears my words and does them, I will show you what he is like: he is like a man building a house, who dug deep and laid the foundation on the rock. And when a flood arose, the stream broke against that house and could not shake it, because it had been well built. But the one who hears and does not do them is like a man who built a house on the ground without a foundation. When the stream broke against it, immediately it fell, and the ruin of that house was great."* (Luke 6:46-49).

Few Christians give Christ permission to lead, chastise, and reveal to them their personal old-nature issues that are often hidden but spring up during a trial or during everyday challenges. Once a hidden old-nature issue is exposed then and only then can it be crucified and replaced with Christlike nature.

This is a narrow-gate and hard-road process that is not magically downloaded or received by the laying on of hands.

The Apostles Paul confirms this process: *"Therefore, my beloved, as you have always obeyed, so now, not only as in my presence but much more in my absence, work out your own salvation with fear and trembling, for it is God who works in you, both to will and to work for his good pleasure"* (Philippians 2:12-13).

What is even more dangerous for the deceived believer is to rely on one's own natural wisdom, strength, knowledge, and spiritual power. These seemingly good inner character traits must also be exposed, crucified, and transformed.

No one, not our pastor, favorite teacher, Bible College, or Seminary can facilitate growing up into Christ, where one's inner person becomes Christlike in character.

Give Christ permission to do what ever it takes to complete his work in you and be willing to follow and obey when he exposes impurities within your heart and spirit. *"Since we have these promises, beloved, let us cleanse ourselves from every defilement of body and spirit, bringing holiness to completion in the fear of God"* (2 Corinthians 7:1).

Therefore, follow Pauls' admonition: *"I appeal to you therefore, brothers, by the mercies of God, to present your bodies as a living sacrifice, holy and acceptable to God, which is your spiritual worship. Do not be conformed to this world, but be transformed by the renewal of your mind, that by testing you may discern what is the will of God, what is good and acceptable and perfect"* (Romans 12:1-2).

The Final Outpouring on the Day That God Acts

What can the sincere saint look forward to in these dark, dreary, and turbulent days? Even though there are many prophesies that this nation will be awakened and be diverted from its self-destructive course—so far, there is no move of God to convert the masses and turn America back to her godly Christian roots.

Everything is getting worse. America and its form of Christianity are on the threshold of unbearable judgments, which will lead to persecution and anarchy.

God is about to act, before the great and terrible day of the Lord. During the coming apocalyptic events, there will be an outpouring of the Holy Spirit upon the hearts of the deceived Christian, the weak, and the lost.

As for the wicked and false believer, their hearts will fall away completely and in pure hatred turn against this last days outpouring and awakening.

A last days awakening is coming that will overshadow all previous outpourings. A holy fear and sense of looming judgment will fall upon millions, and the terror of being left out of eternity will grip masses of confused good hearted people.

Weeping, confessing, repenting, forgiving, restitution, and a holy fear and reverence, in the presence of a Holy God, will fall upon true fellowship meetings. Non-believers and lukewarm believers will be convicted by the Holy Spirit—gasping for breath, weeping and wailing, as they walk down the street, or pull to the side of the road—not by listening to just any sermon.

Without any thought of being religious or just deciding to go to church, scores and scores of ordinary people, doing their daily chores or at work, will fall prostrate before a Holy God and in a dire sense of foreboding fear call out in anguish for Christ to be their savior.

Marked with Relentless Anguish

A broken spirit and broken, contrite heart are God's goals

Rolling waves of weeping and crying-out for forgiveness, in solemn reverence, will fall upon masses in random communities. Individuals and large groups will spontaneously seek help from true servants and workers as they seek understanding and instruction on how to become saved and cleansed by Christ.

The Holy Spirit will fall upon people bringing overwhelming conviction of sinfulness, looming judgment, and the need to become right with God or lose eternity.

There will be no reprieve for individuals—rather a relentless heartfelt anguish that will drive whole groups, communities, and fellowships to their knees and on their faces in dread before a Holy God.

The sincere will weep and pray until they know God has forgiven them. While the hardened in heart will weep for a season and either fake it, becoming deceived by the counterfeit or falling away due to an evil unbelieving heart.

Relief from this impending wave of relentless anguish will not come until true fruit bearing repentance is granted—upon the lost sinner, the self-righteous pew warmer, the backslidden, and the lukewarm believer alike.

News reports will cover these spontaneous acts of contrition as true fellowships burst with new comers and true believers alike.

Those awakened will focus intently on sound doctrine presented by true leadership and will not tolerate entertaining worship or be pacified by shallow messages.

Headlines will trumpet adjective phrases such as: "Phenomenon" "Unexplainable" "Not Normal" "Awe Struck Fear of God" "Solemn Yet Glorious" "The Heavens Opened and Poured."

However, opponents will criticize the awakening as mass hysteria and a fleeting movement of fanaticism. False leaders, out of jealousy, will develop and implement smear campaigns, as they attempt to keep their followers from leaving their flock to find sound fellowship.

While other carnal and false leaders will pretend and act like they knew all about this awakening, even declaring themselves as being used of God to start the final awakening. Some of these false leaders will believe and teach that they fathered the sudden rise of true leaders, with all their prior years of work as prophets or so-called apostles.

Counterfeit Manifestations and False Leaders

The current so-called apostles and prophets, leading much of the Charismatic and Pentecostal movements, will try to slide into the limelight in this coming final outpouring and attempt to hijack what God is about to do.

Satan will attempt to divert this coming awakening in a similar way that he has used time and again, starting with the Wales Awakening in 1904.

Many want to see a great awakening that will start with God's people, then spread to the nation and to the world, resulting in the conversion of America and the world, which will then usher in the return of Christ. These believers want to covert the world because they are unwilling to give up the love of this world.

A great number of Christians firmly believe the body of Christ, through repentance and unity will avert judgment and thus save America. These teachings mislead God's people into ignoring Christ's prophetic warnings of how the end will come and how to get ready to endure to the end and be saved.

This is one the most deceitful teachings of all. This is Satan's trick to keep so-called on-fire Christians sidetracked from the real battle, causing them to ineffectively work in God's final harvest.

These deceived believers will be led by false leaders who purport to walk in the gifts of the Holy Spirit and hold the office of apostle or prophet, operating in signs and wonders. Jesus warns of this end-time work of false movements and false leaders in this passage: *"On that day many will say to me, 'Lord, Lord, did we not prophesy in your name, and cast out demons in your name, and do many mighty works in your name?' And then will I declare to them, 'I never knew you; depart from me, you workers of lawlessness'"* (Matthew 7:22-23).

Counterfeit manifestations will seem to fall spontaneously on many amid this final awakening.

Counterfeiting spirits will attempt to short circuit the process of godly grief, weeping, and the heart felt pain of being unsaved—the Biblical process that leads to true repentance and salvation.

Many who go through this process in this last days outpouring will confess sins in sincere contriteness and will find relief, forgiveness and true rebirth. Pure heavenly joy, rejoicing, and weeping will come upon the truly repentant.

This work of the Holy Spirit is painful, and is God's grace and mercy, and will be dispensed ONLY to the sincere.

Many will cry for salvation but not receive it in the coming wave of this Holy Spirit led awakening. This is where the false leaders and counterfeiting demons slip in, offer false relief, and false spiritual manifestations that may seem joyful but in the end, become damning.

To ensure against a counterfeit hijacking of the final outpouring, the Lord will have set in place His true leaders. The battle to keep the false from sneaking in and subverting this coming final outpouring will be intense.

God will have true leadership arise to manage and protect this coming outpouring, for once again the masses shall clearly see *"the distinction between the righteous and the wicked, between one who serves God and one who does not serve him."*

If this message resonates in your heart in confirmation with the Holy Spirit, then it is God calling you to become a true worker or leader to be trained and used by God during the coming hour—when he gathers in his lost and deceived believers.

God is calling unto himself those who fear the Lord, those who see the hand writing on the wall, to become true bondservants of Christ.

If this is the case for you, then allow God to make you his treasured possession to be spared and used on the day that he acts.

Awakening That Ignites Intense Persecution

Astoundingly, this coming final move of God will not unite America, western nations, or Christianity. This soon to come outpouring will create intense irritation within the hearts of the atheists, the false, and the evil, creating an unbridgeable chasm.

The wicked and the reprobate will not surrender their hope for a new world order and unity through globalism. The masses and most government leaders will reject the call to repentance. Their love of this present age and the pleasures of unrighteousness will grip their hearts, sealing their fate in the coming final harvest.

Though all will witness the final awakening that will astound the world momentarily, the wicked will revolt by trying to destroy this coming work of God.

Many will condemn this true move of God because of the past ridiculous false movements and flamboyant leaders and all the past leaders who engaged in secret sin, corruption, and greed.

There will be many reasons why most of the American and the world's populace will turn against this final true outpouring. The world's rebellion against the Gospel will grow into intense persecution against all true Christians.

The world is in its final battle against its Creator, and the people of the world will not repent of: *"The works of their hands nor give up worshiping demons and idols of gold and silver and bronze and stone and wood, which cannot see or hear or walk, nor did they repent of their murders or their sorceries or their sexual immorality or their thefts"* (Revelation 9:20-21).

Rather, the world will deem true Christianity and Israel as opponents to the world order, prosperity, and peace.

We will soon see what Christ meant when he warned: *"Then they will deliver you up to tribulation and put you to death, and you will be hated by all nations for my name's sake. And then many will fall away and betray one another and hate one another. And many false prophets will arise and lead many astray. And because lawlessness will be increased, the love of many will grow cold. But the one who endures to the end will be saved. And this gospel of the kingdom will be proclaimed throughout the whole world as a testimony to all nations, and then the end will come"* (Matthew 24:9-14).

Lawlessness, Anarchy, and World Order

The Apostle Paul warned of a last day's revolt that will be part of Satan's plan to aid in establishing the antichrist rule.

In the same passage of Scripture, Paul explains that the man of lawlessness will be revealed first, before Christ's coming in the clouds, and that there will be a mysterious rise of lawlessness.

Paul writes, *"For the mystery of lawlessness is already at work. Only he who now restrains it will do so until he is out of the way. And then the lawless one will be revealed, whom the Lord Jesus will kill with the breath of his mouth and bring to nothing by the appearance of his coming. The coming of the lawless one is by the activity of Satan with all power and false signs and wonders, and with all wicked deception for those who are perishing, because they refused to love the truth and so be saved. Therefore God sends them a strong delusion, so that they may believe what is false, in order that all may be condemned who did not believe the truth but had pleasure in unrighteousness"* (2 Thessalonians 2:7-12).

Alarming increases in crime, lawless protests, and political instability are drowning civility all through the American culture. Rancor, hate, and rage are becoming the norm for public debate.

International tensions are reaching all-time highs. The resurrection of the Cold War is hotter than ever, where Russia and China are determined to unseat American dominance and international control.

Wars and rumors of war are a constant threat to global stability. There seems to be no politician or national leader on the global scene that can bring any sense of stability or peace.

The mysterious work of lawlessness that produces chaos and anarchy is no longer constrained. Soon the world will cry out for someone to take charge of the mess, someone who will have answers and the power to bring world peace and security.

The stage is being set for the antichrist to be revealed as the savior for the whole world. The man of lawlessness will somehow be able to demonstrate powerful signs and wonders to gain global compliance.

The antichrist will come, with powers not of this world, to deceive if possible the true Christian.

In Revelation Scripture depicts two "beasts" coming to aid the antichrist in the political takeover of the whole world. The "beasts" will help by demonstrating terrible power, that will convince the peoples of the world to worship these hideous creatures. *(Could it be that these beasts are grotesque fallen angels claiming to be helpful aliens from another planet who have come to bring world order? Pay attention to seemingly ever more creditable ET encounters as Satan grooms the masses to accept the physical manifestation of demons as aliens from another world.)*

God is about to allow multitudes to be deceived and become condemned because of their wickedness. Despite all the truth about the end of this age found in Scripture, a gigantic portion of the world's population will refuse to love and receive the truth. Multitudes will prefer to hold on to the pleasure in doing evil and living in unrighteousness.

The world, in general, is about to be divided into two groups ready for God's final harvest.

The Final Harvests Are Coming

A Harvest of the Righteous and the Wicked

All this is heading towards the final harvests of the righteous and the wicked. In great mercy and wrath, God is about to reap the final harvests of the earth. First the righteous then the wicked.

The Apostle John describes this coming activity of God and his angels as follows:

"Then I looked, and behold, a white cloud, and seated on the cloud one like a son of man, with a golden crown on his head, and a sharp sickle in his hand. And another angel came out of the temple, calling with a loud voice to him who sat on the cloud, "Put in your sickle, and reap, for the hour to reap has come, for the harvest of the earth is fully ripe." So he who sat on the cloud swung his sickle across the earth, and the earth was reaped. Then another angel came out of the temple in heaven, and he too had a sharp sickle. And another angel came out from the altar, the angel who has authority over the fire, and he called with a loud voice to the one who had the sharp sickle, "Put in your sickle and gather the clusters from the vine of the earth, for its grapes are ripe." So the angel swung his sickle across the earth and gathered the grape harvest of the earth and threw it into the great winepress of the wrath of God. And the winepress was trodden outside the city, and blood flowed from the winepress, as high as a horse's bridle, for 1,600 stadia" (Revelation 14:14-20).

Which harvest will you be involved with? Now is the time to give your life without reservation to Christ, and in hunger and thirst seek Him in earnest, while He can be found. He will save, strengthen, and protect those who give themselves to His Lordship, if they hold nothing back.

The time for hesitation has passed!

About Pastor Charles Pretlow and MC Global Ministries

It was in 1973, when Charles accepted Christ, just after his reenlistment in the Marines for six more years. Then in 1974, after reading David Wilkerson's book The Vision, he accepted Christ's call to full time ministry and requested an early release from the Corps. Miraculously, his honorable discharge was granted.

In January of 1975 he began Bible College and accepted his first ministry appointment. His years of formal education and leadership training have helped him in ministry. However, his more in-depth training, wisdom, and character development were honed through years of ministering in a wilderness type training, facilitated by Jesus in the discipline of the Lord.

His call is helping Christians become tribulation proof and rapture ready. Most Christians are not prepared for the coming troubles that God will use to make His church *"without spot or blemish"*—if you will, to become rapture ready.

Contacting MC Global Ministries

If you are seriously looking for sound doctrine to help you get ready and desire genuine fellowship, then perhaps MC Global Ministries and MC Chapel Fellowship may be able to help you.

We mean business and our faces are set as flint concerning the call set before us. If you desire to change the direction God has given us or argue over the message of repentance, sanctification, and how to endure the coming Great Tribulation, then contacting us would not be beneficial.

However, if you are teachable and hungry to learn how to allow the true Christ to change you through his loving discipline, then this ministry can help you.

Ordering Additional Copies

Available online – Amazon, Barnes and Noble
Order at your local bookstore using:
ISBN 978-1-943412-10-5

Contact Information

Mailing address:

MC Global Ministries

PO Box 857, Canon City, CO 81215

(833) 695-1236

www.mcgmin.com ~ contact@mcgmin.com

Fellowship address:

MC Chapel Fellowship

The Abbey/St. Joseph's Bldg.

2951 E. Hwy 50, Canon City, CO 81215

Sunday fellowship 10AM

www.mcgmin.com ~ contact@mcgmin.com

Contacting the author, Pastor Charles Pretlow

PO Box 857, Canon City, CO 81215

(833) 695-1236

Speaking engagement information and requests at:

www.cpretlow.com ~ contact@cpretlow.com